Birch Cottage
and
36 Views of Mount Monadnock

Also by Manitonquat (Medicine Story)

Non-Fiction
Return to Creation
The Original Instructions
Changing the World
Have You Lost Your Tribe?
Ending Violent Crime
The Circle Way
The Joy of Caring for Children

Fiction
Children of the Morning Light
Wampanoag Morning
The Granddaughter of the Moon

Poetry
Grandfather Speaks

Editor
Heritage #3

Birch Cottage
and
36 Views of
Mount Monadnock

by Manitonquat (Medicine Story)

STORY STONE PUBLISHING
Greenville, NH

Birch Cottage and 36 Views of Mount Monadnock
by Manitonquat (Medicine Story)

ISBN-13: 978-1523256570
ISBN-10: 1523256575
BISAC: Poetry / American / General

Story Stone Publishing
167 Merriam Hill Road, Greenville, NH 03048
First printing.

Design: Beechleaf Design
Front cover photo: April Walker
Back cover photo: Ellika Linden

www.circleway.org

Contents

III

Preface

Over forty years ago in a production by the Redwood City Theater I played the part of the Stage Manager in the play *Our Town* by Thornton Wilder. It was a part he conceived of playing himself when he wrote the play, and actually had the opportunity to do so for a Williams College production. So of course I was eager to do likewise myself, as Wilder had been my main inspiration for writing my own plays. I consider *Our Town* and *The Skin of Our Teeth* to be the greatest classics of the American theater. Wilder himself became a friend and mentor to me, and that influence can be seen in my first play, *In the Beginning*, presented by The Community Theater of New York in 1956. Wilder was very helpful to me in my learning and developing my playscripts, commenting in written detail on each version of each play I struggled to write.

Our Town, as I am sure you know, is about the daily life of a New Hampshire town just after the turn of the twentieth century and centering on two families whose houses stand side by side. Wilder developed the script while in residence at the MacDowell Art Colony in Peterborough, New Hampshire. I had not ever been to Peterborough or the area of Grand Monadnock, as the mountain is sometimes called, distinguishing it from a slightly smaller peak in northern Maine and others referred to generically as monadnocks, a coining by a geologist for any mountain that rises as an isolated peak above an eroded level area called a peneplain.

And so I found myself in 1973 standing on a stage in Redwood City California and informing the audience that we were on Mount Monadnock and that down below us lay these towns

Peterborough, Dublin, Jaffrey, and East Jaffrey, little realizing that five years later I would find myself moved with my new family to that very area, living first in Peterborough (Sharon), then Dublin, and later Greenville, where I still reside. Nor that I would resurrect and direct for one season the Monadnock Theater Guild in Peterborough.

In the intervening years I have often climbed the many trails to the summit, trying not too successfully to do so once every year. Like Thoreau and Emerson and countless others, I have found the experience rejuvenating and inspiring. I have tramped up many mountains, in the Great Smokies, in the Rockies, in our state's White Mountains, on Hawaii's Big Island, and Europe's Alps, but the spirit of Grand Monadnock is unique, affecting me as no other. I cannot translate that experience, you must come and climb it for yourself. Not at all hard – it is the most climbed mountain in the world. But I can render this poor tribute, titled in homage to the great Hokusai's prints *36 Views of Mt. Fuji* – the world's second most climbed mountain since they built a road to its summit.

Part One

36 Views of
Mount Monadnock

36 Views of Mount Monadnock

1. From the Hancock Tower in Boston the only
   break in the skyline north and west
   standing guard at the southern
   gates of distant White Mountains

2. From Mt. Wachusett beckoning beyond
   darting and myopic busyness
   a serene healer observing
   all pursuits in tolerance

3. From Hogback beyond the long river
   in Vermont nodding good day
   comfortably in her solitude
   "the mountain that stands alone"

4. From the mists that rise from small lakes
   below her southern aspect she gathers
   herself up her back wrapped
   in sky and thoughtless dream

5. From the window of a log house in Sharon
   where long ago our two-year old son
   announced his latest discovery to us:
   "Look – there's Mount Mon-ad-nock!"

6. From Highway 101 winding down
   the Temple Mountain pass the thrilling rise
   once more of dependable comforting
   guardian of all her sheltered children

7. From college town Keene its commerce
        and distractions a distant reminder
                of silence and solitude and verities
                        not of humankind but of wind

8. From a jet flight out of Manchester
        roaring west over wooded hills
                she rises placid and sedate from below
                        And winks her rocky crest to us above

9. From Ascutney's peak far to the north
        she nods across the hills between
                as if to say "I'm still here holding
                        The line against the southern hordes."

10. Peering down into Jaffrey a vast
        broadside looming over the town
                brimming with possibilities secrets
                        waiting flirting tantalizing

11. Out from her highest parking area yellow
        buses of children hundreds gather
                to assault her easiest trail a few
                        hours from the top of the world

12. Beyond the dappled blue waters
        of Dublin Lake she stretches
                her broad back toward the rocky
                        summit humming to herself

13. From Conval High School in Peterborough
     where the soft shoots of early spring
          stir the blood of yearning students
               unknown desire calling them

14. From the bustling of the summer buzzing
     around the towns she yawns and naps
          and the burgeoning leaves fluffs up
               the forests embracing endless renewal

15. In autumn multi-hued flaming foliage
     down from the north reaching around
          sweeping the lakes running the rivers
               adorned in gold orange scarlet and crimson

16. And from the first snows that cover
     all her slopes and trails, hastening
          our splitting stacking of cordwood
               ready to plow and hunker by the stove

17. And from the summit then a spring day
     leaping across rocks bared by fires
          and erosion a false tree line below
               making our dear old mount a tiny giant

18. All night the full moon listened as we spoke
     On Temple Mountain in circle around a fire
          Of our fathers' harsh distance until the sun
               Struck Monadnock's peak with confidence

19. A lizard on a weather smooth rock
above the tree line embracing
inhaling the wind behind a larger rock
warm in the sun stares and only waits

20. The bare rock of the summit is treeless
here only because the early herders
fired and cleared it and swept erosion
washing it alpine clean to the sky

21. The steepest climb behind us now we rest
and look out to the south falling below
from the Pack Monadnocks to the east past
Watatic and Wachusett to the valley beyond

22. We feel without seeing the long river there
down from the edge of Canada splitting
New Hampshire and Vermont spreading
blessings four hundred miles to sea

23. The peak hidden in a shroud of grey mist
the lakes below blessed by the
fingering waters of renewal
the saltless tears of heaven

24. Around naked boulders April buds
begin to green the skeletal limbs
thirsty arms of winter trees
stretching to breathe spring

25. Last night's snow embroiders the peak
         and treetops with glittering ice
              flashing and winking to find
                   the sleepy blink of dawn

26. Rivulets trickle dripping musically
         rock to rock laughing gushing
              streams together and gossip
                   down the listening crevices

27. No remnant or relic of the first people
         living below along the river Contoocook
              who only came for vision, not to disturb
                   sacred life of the mountain

28. The peaks belong to the small creatures
         too hard for predators to find and worry
              refuge for chipmunk, hare and squirrel
                   alive with snakes, lizards and birds

29. See the ghost of Henry Thoreau down there
         on that promontory, follow him and Channing
              bending spruce into huts and note flora
                   they list tramping together for days

30. And there stands Emerson thoughtful and alone
         Gazing transported in transcendental wonderment
              The intimate community of natural harmony
                   Absorbing him fully in sense and soul

31. Some glimpses of other past visitors marveling
Hawthorne, Kipling, Sam Clemens, Willa Cather
The painters Abbott Thayer and tragic W.P. Phelps
Wilder conjuring life in Grover's Corners

32. On the peaks old winter snows fading gaze at dawn
As rivulets of spring sing down the rocks waken
Violets, trillium, Indian pipes through leaves
Insect, frog, thrush harmonies fill the air

33. Summer unfurls the fiddleheads urging choke cherries
Mountain cranberry, blueberry, wintergreen
Snakes crawl dry creek beds and watchful
Hawks and buzzards circle high warm updrafts

34. In fall mists from still swamps and ponds around the base
below rise where sumac torches burn deep red
Birch and beech above pale to pasty yellow
Sugar maple fires the slopes scarlet and orange

35. Heron and geese winging south through the darkening sky
Grand Monadnock washed cold umber and gray
Returning its world to the long deep night
Quiet under the silent watching stars of winter

36. From the top of nearby Pack Monadnock South
she is like a mother hen spread above
her secret treasures and watching over
all the children of her wide valley

Part Two

Birch Cottage

I

My Gift

I opened my gift this morning
And it exploded me with wonder
Showered shards of heaven on me
That spirit presence that whispers soft
Suspected hidden reality beyond measured
Safety to a thing so distant and deep
It nets me with awe, intimates
Horror and hope, irrational, dumb
Shattering all knowledge and faith, yet
Cradles me firmly in my innocence

The gift I opened this morning
Seems too immense to bear alone
And I crave to share it with you
But how can I, except by word
Nor poetry nor art can hold
That ghost, that presence, only the skin
Pretty as it may be, think you?
If I could tell you, if I could sing
If I could get those colors right
I would open and bathe you in them

But this gift I opened this morning
I can but speechless stare and point
Oh, the leaves, the brave, the sweet, the tender
Dance of gold and ochre, bronze
Burnished, tarnished, blazing light
Cadmium (you see?) before the dark
Patient pines, the columns of ash

Shining birch and how poignant
The gay flutter to cover my garden
To brown and sere and be earth again

A golden ball guards the garden
Attends for me through winter snows
The spring buds, dappled moonlight
Autumn's apotheosis hallowing the woods
In its eye lives holy patient sky
The praying trees, the pilgrim leaves
The sacred glow of earth, my house
Visiting deer, jays and coons
And mystery below, that precious gift:
The opening of my eyes this morning

Slow Down

Let me take you here. Promise – it's good for us both.
Slow down, breathe the birch – the hemlock, pine, ash,
Come back with me now, let's tend to our souls.

Birch Cottage lies back in the woods here
On top of Merriam Hill – from Barrett Road
Spanning the south of the hill you can make out
Far away to the southeast where the sea must be
The towers of Boston struggling for more sky.

From Merriam Hill Road it is a fifth of a mile
Or more than three hundred strides over a rutty
Dirt drive into the woods needing half a dozen
Times a winter to be plowed of snow – some years
It starts in October stays into April – other years,
Like now, teases us warm until the solstice. Seems
More erratic – because of the feared climate changes?

Dave who plows us is from a Finnish family that
Settled in New Ipswich in the late nineteenth century.
He's busy snow time in Mason and Greenville, our town,
But this year his plow broke – he got a friend to do it.
So the walk back is easy, we can drop stress as we go.

My cottage, as I call it, was a small mobile home
Abandoned and rusting all alone when I found it.
A friend who brought it there upped off to Philadelphia,
And it sat deserted for a year when I had to move, and
There it was waiting for me: just three small rooms –

Kitchen in the north end, bedroom in the south,
And a small windowless space in between. It had
Sinks and a toilet and bathtub but no well, no water.

I never dug a well and I still carry all my water in –
Don't have to mess under the house with frozen pipes
At first I had no electricity and no telephone – ah…
Wasn't that a relief! Quiet candle light, lantern light,
A friendly fire from a small cast iron stove, quietly
Chatting, sometimes the hoot of an owl at night,
Or the bustle of small nocturnal critters out and about,
And the chatter of the birds as dawn wakes the woods.

My friends came sometimes to help me build and expand:
A porch; enclosed afterwards for an office; a library –
Book cases floor to ceiling on both lengths; a new roof
To cover the new rooms, with an attic under; a sun deck
Off the library for the company of chickadees and birch;
A much enlarged bedroom; a small den for concentration.
And then, alas and at last, electricity for light, connection:
Computer, modem, telephone answering machine.

I need my work and the connection to the world out there,
But I still carry my water and wood for the stoves –
One in the library, one in the bedroom, but propane
For the kitchen stove and a small electric heater in the den.

After two years Ellika and I met, and she came to help;
Now we spend months making family camps in Europe,
Visiting her Swedish family and neighbors in Copenhagen
Where she also has a home that began as a gypsy caravan.

But life here in our woods slows us to a rhythm of nature,
Lets us watch and listen to the birds and our neighbors
Who are all wild animals. Come and meet them now:
The beavers who build their houses in the pond below;
The otters who play there. The vixen and her cubs
In the hole by the road; the bull moose who moons
After his disinterested mate; the coyote and the bobcat
We only hear cry at night; the deer emerging at dusk;
The porcupines on our deck; the raccoons, red squirrels,
And mice whom we move continually out of our house,
Trap to take and leave by the Souhegan River bank.

We are all attending our guardian Grand Monadnock, carefully
Absorbing its ancient wisdom, learning how to live our time
Together in the mountain's centuries of harmony and grace.

Birch Cottage

My romantic name for this odd little
House, home-grown, hand-made
With a lot of help from my friends,
Built room by room into the woods,
Birch embracing southwest, west, north,
Ash southeast, dark pine to the east.

I love this grove of birch huddling here,
Seeking sanctuary, protection from attack
By the distant army of human busy-ness
That blows its pollution on the wind,
Acid in the rain, affecting these most supple,
Yet most fragile and infirm of trees.

Trees that were sacred to my ancestor's here,
Whose dancing spirits gestured prayers
From Mother's soil to Father's soul.
The clearing was here before the house,
And here we circled for ceremonies
Celebrating the forest and all us children.

Twenty-five years ago I began
Joyously to extend and dismantle
The trailer I wore like a hermit crab,
And now I waken beside my beloved
And watch through the skylight gentle
Fingertips of the sun entwining the top

Fingers of the birches as they sway, then

Through our windows southwest and west
Follow that caress down the white trunks,
The birds and squirrels darting, pausing,
Accepting the forest limits of life
In ceaseless search for nourishment.

Woodland creatures accept my cottage
As part of their habitat. We hear
Strange gnawing in the walls, and mice
Scatter their droppings in drawers and shelves.
Flying squirrels blink from closets, red
Squirrels eat into our food cabinets.

One winter a raccoon had two babies
In the attic (sometimes I had to climb
To ask for quiet while I wrote), wasps
Build homes under the eaves.
A porcupine couple made a baby
Under our bedroom, left him to us.
We fed him that spring until he left home.

Deer watch quietly at dusk behind the trees,
A partridge shoos us fiercely from her nest,
We hear geese bark from their resting
On the pond below the hill where beavers
Work and otters play, and the hunting
Cries of owls and wildcats nightly.

Building a snug fire with deadfall,
We watch a moonlight pavane of birches:
Above the aspiring ghostly trees
The stately procession of the stars.

Into the vast legend of the universe
We praise our home - Birch Cottage.

Come a Bit Closer

I invite you to sit where I am now
Pen in hand, notebook open on my
Very small roll-top desk in my
Very tiny den, electric heater purring,
Breathing to push back the freezing
Wind scratching at the door, the sun
Stroking my left shoulder, peering
At what I write as it dances
Across sparkling crystals of snow
Outside and sketches long shadows
Of birch and ash trees from the woods
Across the clearing to my window
Listen to the cello, organ and
Bass clarinet rumble my stereo
Observe the fallen trellis waiting
Re-instatement after the blasts of winter
Distraught, ragged clouds flee
Across the enigmatic blue above
In hapless disarray the western storm
Soon to deliver more toppings
Of snow on our hills and down
To the waiting maw of the sea

If you sit where I sit, hear
What I hear, see what I see
Papers scattered with notes
Waiting stories longing to be told
The big oaken clock on the wall
Warning with every little leap

Of its hand there are less
And less that I get to tell
Will you see how it is for me?
Will I see how it is for you?
And will that get us close enough
To get through this together?

Meditation

Winter leaks outside
Our bedroom window
A new filled feeder
Sunny seeds and nuts
For nutty nuthatch
Flickadee chickadee
Flitmouse titmouse
Food picker woodpecker
Funko junco
Slow bird snow bird
Shoo jay blue jay
Hard in all cardinal
Now glad for us am I
Together in the world

Remarkable Moments

The public radio afternoon concert
Sending music by Billy Strayhorn
Played on an immense organ through
A small Korean receiver with sub-woofer

Shaking my tiny den (five feet by ten)
Vibrates my chair, rumbling belly to my toes
While outside my window the distant, pale
And yellowing sun spreads creamy light
Across the snow streaked by long slender
Shadows of birch and saplings of ash

Caressing my land, my view, with calm and
Completely natural quiet and confidence
Nothing stirs, the forest holds its breath
Only the shadow of occasional birds
Waft over the snow and blink away

Our ancestors persevered, pounded on logs
Blew through hollow reeds and sent their songs
Through Krishna and David, through Bach
And Blake, through Ellington and Strayhorn
Through Marconi and Edison, mystery, magic

To this moment, to my book-lined, paneled
Den, through speakers on my desk through all
My being, licking scalp, trembling bones
And they are all with me in this moment
We are one. Light on snow and tops of trees

You are with me now here in the moment
Music of our journey, energy, mystery, thought
One remarkable moment after another
Attached to each other strung together
Back to beginning and forward to end

Of time distilled here, all creation
And all of time contained in the moment
Saying to my troubled soul peace
Only notice how remarkable that this
Is you and we are one and all is well.

Rain

Rain. Rain in February. Steady. Slow.
Even. Light. Small droplets thick in the air.
Dimpling my skylight. Soaking the birch woods.
Streaming from the eaves. Purring against
The windows. All last night. All this morning.
And no respite expected tonight or tomorrow.
(Though it may freeze to sleet and snow.)

Heavy with water the sky has descended.
Fog sinks half way down the tree trunks.
Blurring them to a pale gray smudge.
A busy fire talks to itself in my stove.

It feels proper there is too much snow
To be banished by this watery intrusion
Six weeks before the vernal equinox.

But it will clean our old car of salt
And flush out the three hundred meter drive
Through the woods to the state road beyond.

In strange times of warm and cold extremes
Old timers at the diner shake their heads
And recall real winters past, dependable cold,
Digging out from blizzards, knowing seasons
Will revolve in their natural order, but now
We listen and wistfully watch the patient rain
Anxious and aware the arctic ice inexorable
Melts and great rivers thunder through our dreams.

Vernal Equinox 2010

The children are waiting
Elders are listening
Your ancestors are calling you

Can you hear them?
I hear them every hour
When winter stretches

Loosens his heavy coat
And lets it fall drop by drop
From my eaves as now

When dirty drifts recede
Puddles become dark pools
Saplings rise from the mud

Grope for sky and sun
Ascending its gift of days
That will bring us forth

To seeds and tender sprouts
And buds dream and blossom
Come lie upon the back

Of Earth and steer her way
Round and round again
Through eons of stars and tales

Of ancestors singing softly

Leave your confusing cares
Come out and breathe the spring

Your ancestors are calling you
The elders are waiting
The children are listening

April In Our Woods

We are walking out together this morning,
My beloved, twenty years my bride, and I.
She goes to the woods to begin her every day,
Sometimes, as now, prevails on me to come too.
Glad am I she never gives up on me, always
Hopeful, and the gift she is to my days and thought
Forces me sometimes out of myself, to follow her
To the woods, the breathing soul of dreaming earth.
Nights are cold, smoke from the sugar house tells
Maple sap is plentiful now, and the chill of morn
Remains in our eyes to clear and waken them.
Outside our door the blue and white crocus waits
The gentle prod of sun to open again
Rhododendron puts tentative buds to the air.
It will warm soon. The sky is clarion blue.
Green laurel everywhere encourages the spring.
The woods here are varied: slender ash, tall
Silvery beech, much hemlock, some pine,
Old oak. Maple are more by houses and roads,
And hickory are all down the east side of the hill.
Birch are rare and sickly, more sensitive
To the sour rain from the industries to the west,
Their rotting trunks litter the forest floor.
We find a dark freshet warbling deep below
And follow it up again to our neighbor's pond.
Twenty-five years ago he bought the land,
Thirty acres, from our community and eased our debts.
He tore down the houses, built himself a new one,
His own road, and dug his pond below the house.

He is a doctor in the big city and is rarely here,
Only a few weekends a year. We know him little,
Our exchanges all about our spilling over his borders.
Not a country person, at least not a community man,
Not a neighbor as neighbors are reckoned here.
New Hampshire folks are private and possessive too,
So maybe it's the Indian in me wondering about him,
Seems like he knows how to work the culture well,
Property, money, America's model of success.
I'm guessing he toils at undoing the damages of stress
In the city, needs to remove sometimes to the slow,
The quiet, the order and wonder of our woods, dig
His hands in the soil of gardens and watch the ducks.
Well and good. I'm only bothered that during more
Than three hundred days a year his signs warn
Town children not to skate or swim the empty pond.
We lie in sun and watch the ducks – a pair of them
(At least they have not been barred) gliding
Sedately and bobbing for their submerged buffet.
While I plan all I must do today the languid ducks
Just cruise the moment, letting northlands wait:
When the time comes they will be on their way.
Meanwhile mice and squirrels and chipmunks rustle
The dry leaves. In the larger pond below the hill
Mother beaver stirs her mate, "It's half-past
April, time to get busy, the house is a wreck,
The children are famished, the dam leaks,
The otters already out and scouring the pond."
Now the drone of a single plane slices the sky
Like a buzz-saw, reminding both of us
Of the human world beyond that feeds and grows
On its own toxicity, the hunger of its maw

Seeking to swallow every forest, all
Our ash and oak and hemlock, every maple,
Hickory, birch and beech, pine and cedar,
The mice, chipmunks, squirrels, rabbits, deer,
Wildcat, wolf, coyote, moose, raccoon,
Skunk and porcupine, beaver, badger, possum,
Scurrying quail, grouse, turkey and pheasant,
Hawks, eagles, falcons, buzzards keeping watch.
Where will we all go? How should there be life
When April returns but the forest is no more?
I want to tell that pilot up there, all the passengers
Raging the roads of sky and land, come back,
You won't find it anywhere that you are going:
Not peace, nor love, nor freedom, nor joy, nor life –
Nothing your soul requires is there to be found,
Only more search and stress and never April.
Come instead to the woods and follow your love.

Turkeys

Every other day or so the flock
Appears silently mysteriously out of
The dark hemlock trees to the south
Through the sacred birch grove
Bordering, protecting our house
Picking their way slowly silently
In a strange stately dignified file
Outlined against the crusted snow

There are about twenty whose terrain
Seems to be our hill, stalking
The woods and fields from neighbor
To neighbor, their long necks and
Small heads held high looking
Ahead or bending to probe the snow
Scouring the woods like old women
On a barren medieval battle ground
Scavenging any possibility, but moving
Moving, only rarely standing, staring

Then on again following where
The leader has gone and I wonder
If it's always the same leader
Or do they take turns but always
The same route out of the south around
The west side of the house and on
To our neighbor to the north

It's comforting this regular visit

Nice to be sharing the hill the woods
With harmless folk who know no
Borders or boundaries but live
Among us on the hill we all love

Soon I know they will circle around
Bring their ceaseless searching clan
Back close by the house again
And we will feel a surge of joy
To be so honored once more by
Another visit of interesting relatives

Sun Deck 2014

Lying on Birch Cottage deck
In the year two thousand fourteen
Stroked by a musing April sun
Classical Radio Boston wafting
Dreams and moods of Mozart, Bach,
Miracles across the years to this moment
And me in wait under the same
Blue vault and golden orb above

Waiting, with the grass and budding trees
Waiting with the neighbor porcupine
The raccoon, the robin, the chickadee
The turkeys filing through the woods
Every living relative on Earth
Waiting with but a singe purpose

Contemplating the complex moment
Attention fixed, our bodies slipping
Yes my body quietly waits
Not interrupting my attention, lies
Resting, waiting while I wonder
Pondering our future on this planet

My grandchildren and all humankind
Will they learn how to care for it?
How precious they are and how fragile
How much they all need the love
That only they can give to all that is

My Morning Shit

I bury my morning shit in the woods
And the rightness of completion cycles
Allows me pause, coming to rest
Infusing balance, harmony to thought
As well as being.
                    Here's how it works
It's summer, say, as now, patterns
Of the leaves dance in shadow
Into my house through the skylight
Suddenly my bowels know it's time
I enter the woods naked and squat
Sunlight flecks move all about
The earth and my body
                            Evacuating
As my soul is refilled with splendor
Trills of unseen birds in the dark
Undergrowth behind the leaves ablaze
From above, and a partridge drums
Turkeys, squirrels, mosquitoes, flies
Go about their business and I
Finish mine
                My plumbing drained
Still working well (thank you, O Mystery))
I shovel the dirt over, take a deep breath
To absorb my being in the harmony
I am content to know I have made
At least one good contribution
Again today to the great circle.

Composting

I have a simple composting
Toilet, pride of the cottage,

A pile of compost in the woods
Mounting now for decades
Untouched, ready for a garden
That I have no time for, since
At planting time every year
We travel afar in many lands

Planting circles of strangers
Tending and cultivating them
Until they bloom and flourish
As friends to each other and
Themselves, also to the Earth
To seasons, sun, rain and birds

In October we return to the birds
The flaming leaves the quiet woods
And grow the compost pile again
To absorb our commercial breath,
The carbon excreted to choke our air,
And give clean oxygen back to us

My work is just to love all that
Recording all that here for you

More Family

I just went out to our compost pile
To feed it a new infusion of garbage
And there was surprised by a swarm
Of flying creatures I had never seen.
I watched amazed their furious feast
Avidly attacking my smorgasbord
Of rotting veggies and reeking fruits,
Red ocher little dragons hovering
Darting, diving, so many, so close
You'd think they would collide or contest
Each other, but with precise choreography
They executed their ballet prestissimo.

How many of this tribe's relatives are there
Here and around the world, and why
Have I not ever noticed them before?
When my fascination wore off I spread
Wood ashes from our stoves over the pile
Still glistening with recent life, to heat
The stew and hasten the decay,
Food for next year's garden.
The insects departed. Where do they go?
It's a long way from Birch Cottage
To the next compost, and without me
And my waste, how do they survive?

Three Things

Three things
Bring me to life
Every morning when I waken

Her fingernails tracing me
The warmth of her body beside me
One blue eye smiling from the pillow

I stretch in the bed
She moves closer and purrs
I am alive again

Reaching to hold the miracle
We hug and look up
To the skylight over the bed

The tops of birch and ash above
Finger the gentle sky
Morning creeps down their trunks

Seeping into the bedroom
Filling our cottage once again
Our hearts synchronize

Beat together with birdsong
Getting us ready again
                    To live

Autumn Morn

Whirling, spinning across
A chill full moon the dizzy
Dervish leaves dancing wild
Hilarious all night the wind
Stripped nearly bare the lone
Birch outside my window

Replaced on the denuded
Branches as the blushing
Moon retires the pale
Sky now of dawning
By fluttery hundreds
Of small giggly birds

II

December Day

Gray clouds stuck on trees
Drip slow down black limbs
Dappling the old sad snow
Turkeys roost on hickory limbs
Gray squirrels race around
Barren trunks to keep warm
And for something to do

What about the little fox family
Curled in a hole by the septic tank?
The deer huddled under frozen leaves?
Raccoon, skunk pick garbage in town
Possum dreams of snowless south

The birds with strongest wings
Long gone to follow the sun
Sleeping life waits below the crust
The slow months until spring

My love and I open our stove
To reliable balm of burning logs
She addresses a neglected diary

I to my own report: a moment
In one December day now long ago

Frozen Morning

Soft honey light of winter sun
  Strokes the speckled birches
  Through a still and frozen morn

Two gray squirrels chase each other
  Up and down the trees
  A bird just hit our window

Between the vague and inattentive sky
  And marbled snow beneath
  Life flits on frenzied feathers

Gray squirrels, birds and patient trees
  Wonder nor worry not
  At all beyond present need

Spring holds no hope nor winter fear
  For them no time nor wish –
  As it is – is all there is

Folly to dream there should be more

From My Journal

On our bed, my beloved and me
Reduced to essence, succor, safe,
Soft asylum, nesting hidden, home
Free together, ultimate ground,
Where we begin and end each day,
Eat, sleep, copulate, muse
And dream, now we write and probe,
Scratch our longing and share reports
Of sojourns into wild terrains
Unknown to us and everyone.

I glance across at her, moving
Her pen bemused over the page,
The nub striking bold marks unlike
The thin careful embroidery of
My own marbled Pilot pen (extra fine).
Feeling my glance she reflects a smile
Beaming through her concentration out of
That unbroken flow of love that glows
From her source and nourishes me.

A sudden ache of gratitude snags
Inside me for her dear vast heart
That grieves and rejoices for all life
Unerring in allegiance to every being,
Most particularly the small, the weak,
The suffering, the mute and voiceless,
The innocent, the wronged, the oppressed,
Whatever is hurt or struggles to be free.

Moments ago a small bird flew
Slam into our windowpane,
Stunned, unmoving a time, in which
She worried for its head, its wing,
And ten minutes later rejoiced
To find it flown away and gone.

What a precious gift to feel and share
And gasp together in the poignancy
And the glory of the woods and fields
Of this hill acknowledging distances:

Temple Mountain and Pack Monadnocks
To the north, quarries of Milford to the east,
Southeast the faint towers of Boston,
Southwest the ski trails of Wachusett,
Below the hill the chattering scramble
Of the little Souhegan River busily
Pouring the sky through dappled woods.

Recognition of identical delight
In trolls by John Bauer or cello suites
Of Bach or the humane humors
Of Astrid Lindgren, or a rimmed moon
Rising with the sun beyond the sea.

Our minds together grant intimation:
The unity and the mystery of it all.

Andover Cemetery

(A 1967 poem rediscovered in 2015)

Climbing the hill in morning mist
Hanging about the thick green that cradles
The winding narrow Shawsheen River
Sounds are the same after twenty years
And more: occasional hum and hiss
Of motor cars on unseen roads,
Thrushes piping, bluejay's screams
And the endless immemorial hollow
Calling of crows across the wood,
Setting each other off, like watchdogs.
The gravestones are as still
Mysterious, non-committal,
Unavoidable, unmistakable, indifferent
As ever, only many more now.
Another familiar sound: the hoarse
Muffled whistle of the Boston and Maine
Leaving town, shaking and swaying
Into sight briefly along the cemetery,
Swallowed again in wood and mist,
Silence, and the call of birds.

Whoever cleared the cemetery had
The good sense to leave the oaks –
A half dozen old individualists
Whose assorted deformations reflect
The strength of lone and tough, bent
And cranky New England character.
Some of the stones too shiny and sharp;

Weather has a cure for that.
The little imported cedars too perfect,
Like the potted geraniums, well,
Give them time, they'll bend and rot
And finally fit in with our temper.
From bronze American Legion stands
Little banners caress the air –
So many tiny stars and crimson stripes
Softly gesture with frivolous grace
Among the rows of moveless stones.

More than twenty years ago I came
With my schoolmate Fred to watch
Autumn emblazon the valley,
Smoke our pipes and listen,
Read poetry, philosophize.
If he were here now probably
We would only listen and smoke.
But I am alone and these oaks,
These flags, geraniums and cedars,
These thrushes, crows and angry jays
Amid the unmoved unmoving stones
Make me wish a woman with me,
Some gentle enigmatic female
Fellow sojourner among the mysteries
With quiet smile and fathomless feelings
Who would nevertheless dance with me
Naked among the blind stones, dumb flags,
And make love on the cool wet grass.

Caves In the Jetty

I recall those rocks those great
Gray granite boulders piled
Over each other a muscled forearm
High enough to stand above
Tide and wave in every weather

Myself a boy leaping the length
Of breakwater sheltering the only
Tiny harbor basin affording
Haven along that sandy coast
Springing sure-footed rock to rock

Hiding in their damp mysteries
Caves and crawl-spaces, tunnels
Labyrinths of other magic
Under ocean below mind
But mine alone, only mine

How small they seemed, the rocks, caves
That hidden world when I returned
A man, a father, with my sons
Who found them all, my hidden rooms
Explored their secrets every one

I see my youngest as myself
Brown skinny limbs spidering
Into crevices, black eyes flash
Under shadow cracks connecting us
Ancient spirits of rock and sea

Now they are men too large
For the shrinking magic tunnels
Cryptically viewing a vanished world
When were we boys. Now I wait my
Grandchildren to regain the cryptic wonder.

Here I Stand

Here I am. Here I stand
Surrounded by more books
Than I can ever read even
If I read all day every
Day the rest of my life
Looking at stacks and stacks
Of letters to answer, tax forms,
Bills, notebooks, scraps of ideas
For more work than I can ever finish
In this lifetime, with a refrigerator
Full of dried and bearded cheese
Wilted spinach, souring milk, leftovers
I'll have to throw out one of these days
An attic full of yellow newspapers
Drafts of articles, stones, diaries
Piles of photographs of trips and people
I've forgotten, my wallet full
Of old business cards and phone numbers
I don't recognize or remember at all

A house full of stuff gathering
For years and I don't know
Where I have put anything
And wonder if that is old age creeping
If death, that trickster, is sneaking up
Through all this stuff on me
I wonder what is this death?
Being dead. But then there is no "be"
Is it just this forgetting, only complete?

I say, like most people, I think
I must be losing my mind, but what
Was my mind when I had it?

I turn up the stereo, soak my senses,
(I have more recordings than I could
Ever listen to). Outside the French doors
Snowflakes whirl in the sun and quiet
The eager sprouts below the crusted earth
On the deck the chickadees race the squirrels
For the sunflower seeds I have broadcast
Mozart laughs and plays his endless song

For a brief instant I shudder in the truth
Of the ineffable connections that weave us all
Suns and space and squirrels and snowflakes
And I, not at all like Luther,
Determined and sure of his theses,
I, only a bit bewildered but still alive,
Here I stand, here I am.

I Don't Want to Go There

NO NO NO NO, NO, NO,
Take it away, turn it off.
I don't want to go there.
No more World News Tonight.
Throw out the TV, smash the radio,
Light the papers in the stove for tinder,
Stop all my subscriptions today,
The lies, the follies of all the nations,
Sinister patterns of greed and malice,
The design of grinning corporations
Black holes of venal avarice,
Sucking more and more into horror
And oblivion, unreality, reversing creation.

It's up at the road now, whining, filling
My mailbox with artful seductions.
Keep it out of my sacred woods,
I don't want to go there.

Just let me stay among the guardian
Pines, the devoted hemlock, here where
The tall ash and birch are smiling
And sheltering our forest home,
Every morning watching the titmice,
The chickadees and nuthatches taking
Turns at our feeder, different families
But a regular little tribe together.
The blue jays and cardinals keep
An aloof and envious distance until

The feeder is free of small flittery things.

No, don't tell me, stay away,
I don't want to go there,
Where brain-beaten boys grimly
Belt themselves in dynamite to herd
In their hatred the chattering women
Haggling in the market, a black hole
Whose edges are blood and screams;

One gray squirrel, my favorite,
Is hanging by his tail on the swinging
Feeder poking at the seeds to make them fall
To his accomplice working the ground
Freezing now and then to check me out
From profile or darting up a tree and back

No I won't go there, not there
Where children creeping to the well
To bring water for huddled families
Are snatched by foaming fuming men,
Torn, raped, and tossed in the trash;

I'm just going for a little walk –
Watch that partridge come racing out
Right toward me, leading me away
From her nest in the dark undergrowth.
I play a game and run down the path
And she faithfully follows, wings

Flapping as she runs, brushing the leaves.

Partridge, can't we just stay with you, run
With the turkeys, the coons, foxes, the deer?
Invite our family of troubled Earth to come
And live in harmony, grace, and gratitude?

Sometimes

Sometimes – not often – but every now and again
I find myself wishing a more complex intellect
People think me really smart, and so I am
So are you and all when we attend and care
We have a cortex that snaps and slashes speedily
Sees to essences, cuts corners and frills and seizes
On the nub with sound conclusions and decisions
But I must admit there are times while reading
This or that philosopher, scholar, pedant, this literary
Critic or analyst I shake my brain in awe
At their distinctions, complications, nuances
Of original, provocative reason, and I'm obliged
With head sore and reeling to stumble out
Beyond myself. Knowing my cleverness never
Will bring me to this new geography, I may
Sometimes envy those complex weighty thinkers.

But then I see the moon above my cottage skylight
Fiercely staring down a starry vault above the trees
Mozart alive through my radio from Symphony Hall
Fills my brain with an exhilaration of exquisite joy
And in deathless complete perfection I breathe
My life, my hours, moments of learning, playing
Writing, loving my lovely companion, my family,
Friends, all in a balance so delicate and fine
I dare nor pray not the least otherwise – for this
O moon! O Mozart! O life! That all this should be!

Too Much

Now what? It's all too much.
My desk overflows, baskets
To be filed, closets stuffed,
Drawers too full to close,
I can't find anything.
I'm drowning in acquisition.
Too many books I want to read
And only stare at all those covers.
Too much music to choose to hear.
I dare not watch the news.
Too much horror and misery.
Hundreds of magazines want
To teach more than I care to know,
Beckon me to Samoa, Machu Pichu,
Toscana, Aruba, Bratislava,
The Seychelles, see Naples and die.
The forest outside is glistening
Rainbow diamonds of ice
The sky too blue, the sun too
Loving – it's all too much
Except time – get rid of time
I want it all now. All.

Notes to Thoreau

Hi, Henry. Here's how it looks now.
Those quiet desperation folks?
They are staring at their TVs,
Exacting mayhem on computer games,
Talking loud non-stop on mobile phones
Retailing vacuous inanities to fill the time,
Creating fantastic lies of romance and
Internet adventure in crowded cyberspace,
Swallowing pills to get to sleep, pills
To stay awake, pills to ease the stress,
Pills to hold an erection, pills to counter
The side effects of all those pills, buying
Into the latest therapy, the newest path
To enlightenment or bliss, to lose weight
Or stop losing hair, rushing to the mall
To load up with whatever is on sale
Filling their houses with junk they will forget
Until they display it at their next yard sale.

I'm glad you came and left when you did.
It was bad enough that the train came by
Then just above Walden every day – now
It passes many times morning till night,
And nearly every minute the sky above shudders
With Boston's relentless air traffic to and fro.
You had not to imagine the chemical slime swirling
Where you paddled the Concord and Merrimac.
No more come by horse or carriage to walk
The sands of Cape Cod's Atlantic arm –

Now a thousand cars block the bridges.

Different even when I was a boy seventy years
Ago and a hundred later than your journals.
We had no Cape highway, no motels,
Shopping centers, New York shops, fast food,
Fast cars, fast lanes, fast books, fast money.
The Cape beaches sinking with people and trash.
In nineteen thirty-four I read a new book
By the Cape's favorite author, Joseph C. Lincoln,
In which he limned sketches from his youth:
A Cape you approached by boat or stagecoach,
Where shopping for utensils or sharpening tools
Was from a cart that passed each house each month,
Where blizzards meant you stoked the fires to wait
The week cozily by your hearth for roads to clear –
How silent, how slow, time for thinking and talking,
For the completeness of reflective living.
Joe Lincoln lamented the natural pace of the Cape
Banished by the noise and stress, the nineteen thirties –
A time I recall as gentle and slow, the milkman
Delivering bottles to our door, the ice man bringing
Blocks from our frozen lake to fill the icebox top,
The sweet fisherman offering his catch, happy
I loved the butterfish few others cared for.
In summer the people sharing the beach, children
I built sand castles with, all were neighbors,
And I could run naked and free behind the dunes.

Henry, you don't want to see it now, Route Two
Past Walden clogged with commuters weaving
Into and out of the city, beaches crushed with bodies

Smelling of sun cream and insect repellent stepping
Over each other, a stew of cell phones and boom boxes.
The Maine woods fill up with motor homes,
Connecticut Indian casinos chatter and clatter greed,
The rich steal from the government, corporations steal
From the earth, and the poor steal from each other.
America's major industries are the military
And the prisons. You refused to pay
For Mr. Polk's war with Mexico, how say you
To Mr. Bush's pre-emptive invasion for oil?

Well, Henry, like you I can maintain sanity,
Confront essentials, and reflect on madness
In my hand-made cottage in the woods, where
I carry water, chop wood, talk to the birds,
The squirrels, raccoons, porcupines, who share
My food and shelter. Like you, Henry, I
Will leave my testament and be glad I won't
Be here to see the worst. And should we meet
Wonder what more we could have said or done.

III

Disaster

We heard the cracks like gunshot
Exploding above us all night long,
My beloved and I, clinging together
In apprehensive wonder, waking
To find our cottage surrounded, embraced
By our familiar guardians fallen
Faithful upon their last battleground,
Lying still beside us entombed in ice.

Our sacred birch grove laid low
In the night by weight of water, ice
Layering ice, embracing clinging,
Encasing every twig and limb
Until the heaviest and tallest succumbed
And one by one, the soil and roots
Unable to bear them longer, the noble
White giants toppled and sank to earth.

I envy my beloved wife, who sat up
And screamed at the first sight and wept
Wringing, copious tears and wailing
Our shattered woods, the lovely cadavers
Of white trunks and branches lying
Tangled helpless about the house,
Grateful too that she can weep,
Shedding tears enough for both of us.

The lowering sun now ignites
Thousands of tiny gleaming sparks

On the frozen limbs that weave
Around the windows, a crystal forest
World freezing the time to memory.
I am frozen too, bewildered, numb,
Unfeeling, stunned, groping for what
May let me enter this alien world.

Having been nurtured by the birches,
The decimation of the grove strikes us
Vitally, paralyzing the normal function
Of my brain, I wait the return of reason,
Wishing meanwhile I had the poetic power
Of a Milton, a Hardy, a Yeats, a Frost,
To convey the range of this disaster
But sing I must for our sake as friends.

The hours pass, the day passes.
The night releases us, covers the tragedy.
A blink in the sky wobbles – that is
No star, no plane – now there are more:
They are sparkles of ice drops lit
By the full moon, the dark wind
In trees above our skylight waving
Back at pale clouds racing the night

Now it is morning, the second morning
Of a new, strange, inchoate world.
Nothing has changed, time still frozen
Sunlight strikes to blinding brilliance
The millions of crystal drops blazing
The forest grove, colors flash within
Death's beauty with irresistible radiance,

Piercing all with the splendor of now.

I am, we are all, here to learn –
What do I take from this unexpected
Cataclysm that has torn out the
Heart of woods thirty years my home?
Only the giants fell, the ones that grew
Too tall for the soil to support – the lesson:
The higher we aspire to heaven, the deeper
Must we thrust our roots into the Earth.

How am I to comprehend this deluge of ice?
As custodian of the woods where lies my task?
Is it to realize the logic and rightness of death?
Rebirth and renewal – new woods from old.
With gratitude in mourning we must care now
For our vanquished elders, restore the grove
To new life and the hope of seeds,
Seedlings and saplings, reaching to the sun.

Rehab Dreaming

It's been almost three months now –
I have grown used to the sight of devastation.
In two weeks spring will be here,
Sequan dancing in and with the warm
Breath of his flute banish lingering snow
From the morning windows of our bedroom
I count thirty birch either on the ground
Or leaning broken and bent beyond recall.
The snows have kept us from moving them
So we live among our dead companions
To become one with the forest, accepting
Its need to bring new health, clean
The overcrowded earth and bring in wind
And sun for the new growth struggling.
We inhabitants, squirrels, birds, and others,
Must make the best of this recuperation.
As caretakers we will do our best to help.
The time to mourn is past, now we gather
Our dreams, our seeds, sprouts and saplings
To make fresh the family, strong and new.

What to Do When Stuck

How's it going? You ask. Honestly?
Hard. Just now. It doesn't go at all
Like the old cars I used to have
It doesn't go unless you push it

Midway on the path of life I paused –
Well, not midway of course, I sailed on
Past that – I count the years in scores now
Four score and so much more to do

But I'm stalled. Do others find it
This hard just to move in the morning?
Lying in my bed, my cells rebelling
Body dead weight, mind cleared out

Flames through my stove window flick
Their red tongues around the birch logs
Eating slowly the remnants of the storm
Comforting. The sun has more room now

To wade the crumpled woods beyond the window
The squirrels race on broken birches
(Lying, standing, leaning). The little birds
Flutter and dart among confused branches

Now that small red squirrel sitting still
On a thin twig, curled ball of fur wrapping
His tail over him like a quilt against the wind
Staring. Does he think? Does he wonder?

Kwan Yin from her little shrine looks down
Musing sadly, pouring her compassion
Endlessly out to the ravaged world beyond
Listening to Bach mourning from my stereo

Okay, I'm still in bed, but at least
I'm sitting up, my hand and pen moving
Going with my thoughts, so that's progress
Right? Take one breath at a time

Now from the kitchen sounds of breakfast
Being made, poetic aroma of coffee
Brewing, the fuel and armor prepared
To enter once more that damaged world

My sweet companion, also damaged, still
Singing, ministers to my life and to all life
With such love she gets stuck too like me
Bewildered by it all, the damaged world

But in her love she is never confused, she is
Love pure and simple. She awakens my love
Plucks me from confusion. Having each other
We have it all, nothing to do now but love

At the Ruins of the Shrine

It is more than a year now since
That straining blizzard that, like blind
Sampson, brought this temple down,
The white branched pillars which stood
Here stretching high for bless of sun
Lie still broken and shattered, relics
Of an ancient holy sanctuary, containing
Arcane mysteries I could only praise.

Feeling my impotence, unable to rebuild
The sanctum sanctorum, felled not
By man (acid rain may be complicit)
But by our wise Mother, to clear the thicket,
To air it out, to prepare her nursery for
New growth in her womb under the snow.

I have not the strength to dissever the limbs,
Hew, chop, slice, cleave, split cadavers
And carry the pieces to stack the cords
For my stove against New England winters.
All I, ineffectual caretaker, can do
Is pay a morning homage, the low sun
Slanting to bless these crippled servants
Of the enigmatic holy order we all obey.

Hope In the Forest – the Return

I return from spring and summer pilgrimage
As the raging flames of splendid autumn
Crumple to leafy brown carpets blanketing
Fallen rotting cadavers of birch elders
The cottage roof leaking untended still
Alive for another somnolent winter
Enough wood split and stacked
To warm and dry the library and bedroom
Time now before the snows descend
Restore order to the kitchen and the study
Feed the chickadees, nuthatches and titmice,
And somehow fit the life of our woods
The birch, ash, hemlock, hickory, pine
The porcupine, raccoon, deer, fox and lynx
The turkeys in their stately tribal wandering
Into the clamor of a raging tragic outside
World of uncontrolled mass destruction
Murder, terror, horror: vicious, dumb, bitter
Blind, inhuman genocide of animals and trees.
We feed our furred and feathered family
Nurture hope again somehow life will prevail
And know the forest and breathe its seasons

Keeper of the Woods

A gray day outside our windows
As autumn pauses its festive dance,
Its painted leaves shiver and wait
The urging of the next wind to beckon.
The birch grove diffused in glow,
Pale and gold without source or shade,
Vague and mystical, breathing magic.
A vine has crawled across the arch
Of our trellis, staking its territory,
Here to stay. Many birds have fled,
But chickadees and their companion
Nuthatches and tufted titmice
Have permanent residence, dropping in
To our feeder for their share of seeds.
Strange to think we are more than just
Denizens of this grove, nesting here,
More even than just protectors,
We are actual owners of the land –
Absurd concept! Owning our own Mother!
But there it is. Society insists,
The neighbors, the town, the human race
All insist on human ownership.
So that it might not succumb
To human development, clear cut,
Bulldozed for housing, colonial or cape,
Garages, drives, complexes, condos,
Or another mobile home park,
I must become an owner, a role
I never wished, mortgage and deed

Duly registered and appraised
For tax to serve community needs.
But strive I must to hold these woods,
These delicate birch, hardy ash and pine,
Vigorous hemlock, succulent sugar
Maple and our thriving inhabitants
The deer, raccoon, woodchuck, rabbit,
Bob cat, Bobwhite, partridge, pheasant,
The warblers, thrushes, orioles, owls,
Blue jays, cardinals, crows, black birds,
The herd of turkeys and the singing frogs,
Innocently all somehow depending on me
To sort the demands of my careless species
For the generations we shall never know.

Back to Monadnock

Back to Monadnock
        Where shall I die?
Beneath the fallen birch?
        Squirrels leaping over me
Chickadees flocking with their tribe
        Nuthatches and titmice, or
Before my stove watching the flames
        Lick old memories of days
Faded, worn, and dim but softly felt?

Today I got out an album to show
        My son to his wife, how he was
One photo showed me thirty-eight
        Years ago kissing the tears of
My two-year old looking just like
        Him with my grandson today

Day dreaming the closing hours of a life
        Is not as much fun for me
As reliving passions unattainable
        A forgotten appetite for pain

I cannot resurrect, heal or restore
        The fallen loveliness of the birch
Nor can they heal me altogether
        But we live on together

Rooted in the soil ancient glaciers turned
        Cultivating the tender sprouts
Seeking growth from seeds
        Scattered through my life and mind

Reasons to Be Here

They're back! Our sweet porcupine family
Is back, nibbling seeds on our deck again – oh
I wish you could come and see them now!
There are four tonight. We turn the light
On outside – it does not concern them at all.
They know us well. Many years ago
We heard them first at night, right under
Our bedroom. It was only mama and papa
Then, the squeals of their copulating
A happy music to our cuddling above.
Later a baby emerged with them on the deck,
Which soon they left to our care and departed.
Over the years one, two, or three returned
After every summer.
                    Winter came late this year –
No porcupines. But now, in a frigid January,
They are back. We don't know which are parents,
Which mates, or siblings, but they belong here:
One is on our chair, probing the table, one climbs
The post. Ellika brings new seeds and apples –
They accept her sitting and watching. Two of them
Touch noses together and squeak happily –
They are content. They are home. They take
Whatever the world offers – us included.
Thank you, forest world, for all our family:
The birds, the turkeys, foxes, bobcats, squirrels,
Raccoons, deer, moose, hares – we have reason
To care and go on together in our time on Earth.

About the Author

Manitonquat (Medicine Story) is a storyteller, an elder and a keeper of the lore of the Assonet Band of the Wampanoag Nation of Massachusetts. Author of ten published books and a former columnist and poetry editor with the internationally acclaimed journal *Akwesasne Notes*, he has also edited *Heritage*, a journal of Native American liberation. He continues to develop tools for creating a more humane society based upon teachings of the elders of the First Nations and the explorations of his camps under the designation The Circle Way. They have a website at www.circleway.org.

Manitonquat has spoken to peace conferences and groups on three continents, was the keynote speaker at the United Nations observance of the 50th anniversary of Gandhi's assassination, directs prison programs for native spirituality, advises a nature school, and, with his wife Ellika, makes workshops and annual international family camps and advises new communities in ten European countries and the US.

CPSIA information can be obtained at www.ICGtesting.com
Printed in the USA
LVOW12s1526100316

478624LV00007B/864/P